PRAISE FOR *LIF*

"I was stopped in my tracks reading your poems, taking in the Living Rumiesque potency of your words in service to the One."

—Candace Freeland, photographer, musician, Black Mountain, NC

"Unexpected truths; wide-open heart; beauty on every line."

—Cindy Buck, author, *Chicken Soup for the Gardener's Soul,* Fairfield, IA

"*Life as a Prayer* is a gentle and potent invitation into the landscape of the soul's journey as it seeks the light in the field of life. Jennifer's timeline takes you by the hand and slips you into breathless states of your inner Nature. You will find it simple and sublime."

—Lilli Botchis, PhD, author, *Awakening the Holographic Human,* Vero Beach, FL

"Each poem is a whole world and a beautiful gift . . . everything great poetry should be."

—Margaret Glazer, reader, Fairfield, IA

"Your poetry captures a pure essence of soul-felt reflections evolving into a transcendent peaceful elysian sanctuary. We really loved it and will enjoy reading it again and again."

—Rob Mancheri, DC, Smithville, NJ

"My granddaughter keeps asking me if I believe in God . . . . I will read her 'Easter Morning on Black Mountain' and 'The Beauty of Him.' Maybe they will help her understand."

—Kendy Madden, writer, Durham, NC

Thank you for touching my life with beauty, and grace, and meaning."

—Linda de Graaff, reader, Louisville, KY

LIFE AS A PRAYER

OTHER BOOKS
BY JENNIFER READ HAWTHORNE

Chicken Soup for the Woman's Soul
(with Jack Canfield, Mark Victor Hansen and Marci Shimoff)

Chicken Soup for the Mother's Soul
(with Jack Canfield, Mark Victor Hansen and Marci Shimoff)

A Second Chicken Soup for the Woman's Soul
(with Jack Canfield, Mark Victor Hansen and Marci Shimoff)

Chicken Soup for the Single's Soul
(with Jack Canfield, Mark Victor Hansen and Marci Shimoff)

Diamonds, Pearls & Stones
(with Barbara Holden)

The Soul of Success

Life Lessons for Loving the Way You Live
(with Jack Canfield and Mark Victor Hansen)

LIFE AS A PRAYER

— POEMS —

JENNIFER READ HAWTHORNE

For Karen,
with love and blessings

First Edition: June 2019
Printed in the United States of America
ISBN: 978-0-578-58841-4
Cover Design: M.H. Pasindu Lakshan

High Tea Press
5035 Fairways Circle, #306
Vero Beach, Florida

Ripening

Fullness is on me
like the taste of watermelon in summer.
My remaining days stretch out
like a carpet of ripe pecans
on the floor of the orchard
behind my grandparents' house,
each one waiting to be
picked up, cracked open, savored.
No more youthful hunger;
I eat the moonrise over the ocean,
my mouth round with silver.

CONTENTS

3. SIMPLE THINGS

LIFE AS A PRAYER

1

BLOOD AND EARTH

I was born in Baton Rouge, six blocks from the Mississippi River and straight into a Huckleberry Finn childhood. I spent my youth riding ferries back and forth across the river, intoxicated by the smell of earth and flowers: honeysuckle, gardenias, magnolias, mimosas, white clover.

My father had been killed six weeks before my birth; he was on his way home from work at Exxon's Baton Rouge refinery when a truck driver ran a red light and struck his motorbike. He died instantly. But his parents and brothers stayed present for my mother—an immigrant from England—and for my two little half-sisters, born later to my mother and her new husband, my father's best friend, whom she married when I was eighteen months. We ate watermelon on my grandmother's back stoop in the hot summers, fetched eggs from the chicken coop, and played for hours under my grandfather's award-winning camellias.

But things fall apart. Families change. Greed and jealousy are potent influencers. Years later, I had to learn where to look for family, how to make a broken heart whole again. I had to learn how to put down roots in places far from home.

Close to the Ground

We children lived close to the ground.
We noticed mud and fire ants,
low-hanging nests,
fairies on toadstools.

The earth was our lover.
We rolled in the velvety ryegrass,
somersaulting, cartwheeling
our way through summer.
We sat in the clover,
wove white-pink blossoms
into crowns for our princess heads.

We drew hopscotch grids in charcoal
on the driveway—
jump-straddle-jump-straddle—
our feet dropping
into the hollow spaces.

We resisted dusk's call to supper,
pleading for one more dance
with winking fireflies
around the bridal veil.

And when at night we fell asleep
and dreams lifted us,
we were unafraid to leave the ground,
still covered in green
and the smell of the sacred earth.

Night's Playground

I cartwheel a hundred times across the lawn,
going for a new world's record.
My body arcs and arches
into circling backbends, flowing walkovers.
I hurl myself into back handsprings,
vaulting around the yard on confident bones.

Across the street, behind Miss Kitty's gable roof,
the moon peeks out, begs me to wait for her.
Hurry, I urge, willing her to rise higher, faster,
but my mother's voice cuts through the twilight
from the kitchen window.

Too late, Moon comes out of hiding,
throws down her light, dares me
to take center stage on the driveway.
Quickly, I perform my best arabesque,
stretching gracefully from fingertips to toes
before twirling my way to the side door,
where reluctantly, I relinquish the day
to the night keeper
of my dusky playground.

The Delta

Let's go down to the levee, my father says,
and three squealing girls tumble
into the backseat of our '57 Chevy,
headed for the Mississippi
and the wide-open space of Sunday afternoon.

Three little hearts race as we crest the levee,
then, like a river, roll down the other side
straight into our own Huck Finn adventure—
people, cars, stray dogs swarm the landing,
twin ferries crisscross the river.

The old ebony preacher man stands thigh high
in the dark muddy water,
wrapped in white sheets, stick cross in hand.
We edge closer to my father,
relief that we're already baptized washing over us.

At the ferry's blast, we scramble
up three flights of stairs to the highest deck,
eyes wide at the tugs and barges,
massive ships bulging with Louisiana oil,
cars loading below like Legos, bumper to bumper.

We race to the lower deck,
hang over railings, faces close
to whirlpools and eddies,
as Father clutches at three little waistbands.

The river is wide at Baton Rouge,
plenty of time to savor the crossing.
I find an empty bench,
lie down and close my eyes.

The Southern sun is warm on my face,
the engine *chug-chugs* beneath me,
the river rushes wildly toward New Orleans,
hungry for freedom.

I understand its longing.
I was born on this river.
The delta is my home.

Panther Girl and the House of Windsor

1.

My china cabinet is soft, pink wood,
with latticed glass-paned doors.
It holds kings and queens,
tea parties and dinners,
aunts and great-grandmothers.
It speaks of ancient empires,
God Save the Queen,
the perfect cup of tea.

Next to the napkin rings,
the cream-colored gravy boat perches.
Cake plates on pedestals converse easily
with creamers and sugar bowls,
painted flowers, fluted edges,
twelve place settings of the wedding china.

Through the glass, members
of the House of Windsor look out
at the silk and wool Persian rug,
the dining room table made
of gold-flecked iron and glass—
the perfect dining room
where no one ever eats.
No mismatched pieces here,
but Charles and Diana have started to crack.

2.

High up in the mimosa tree in the backyard,
Panther Girl yawns and stretches herself
full length on her favorite branch.
She is sleek and black,
fierce and fearless,
content in her tree.

3.

When I was five,
Prince Charles and his princess sister
held a place of honor
in my pink plastic wallet.
In England, my British colonel grandfather
tended his small green garden,
trained me not to be seen.
But down the road, Mrs. Cook let me sit
at the table with the grownups at teatime,
drink my tea from a china saucer
with a silver teaspoon.

4.

At three, I stand on a chair in the kitchen
in red-and-white flannel pajamas,
stirring the Christmas pudding
with a wooden spoon.
Mummy boils shillings and silver dimes
to add to the mix,
which we will eat Christmas Day—
like it or not—just to find a shiny coin
that promises good luck.

Years later my mother gives me a cake platter
—the pedestaled one—with a matching cake server
covered with flowers and vines, gilded edges.
Never mind I haven't baked a cake in thirty years—
It looked like you, she says.
You can never have too much china,
my sister adds.

5.

From the mimosa tree,
Panther Girl imagines cries
from her doll-baby children
in the playhouse below.
In a single leap, she reaches the ground,
enters the house to find her children
demanding their tea.
She puts the kettle on, sets the table
with her turquoise and gold tea set,
her very own since four.

Picking up her babies one by one,
she holds them close,
tosses them into the air.
"Cake or biscuits?" she asks,
but settles for bread and marmalade,
scones with double Devon cream.
"Delicious!" she cries,
and everyone agrees.

She kisses her babies,
declares it's naptime.
Certain they are sleeping,
she closes the door softly.
Bare feet hug smooth bark
as she climbs back into her mimosa world,
stretching lazily, languid on her branch.

She lays her face close
to a cluster of soft fringe petals,
as pink-blossom nectar smells ride
her breath in and out.

Huck Finn and Me

Anybody who wasn't born there thinks the Mississippi River is a slow moving, lumbering thing, just "rolling along," as the song says. But I can tell you that by the time Ol' Man River gets to Baton Rouge, he's in a hurry. He can smell the coffee and beignets at the Café du Monde, taste the promise of the Gulf of Mexico.

Ask Daddy and Uncle Frank, who thought they'd paddle a canoe from Memphis to New Orleans when they were young, just for kicks. Lucky to make it thirty miles before the whirlpools spit them out instead of drowning them.

That river has seen a thing or two. The most fun I ever had was the night my boyfriend and several other college crazies set his old Morris Minor on fire and pushed it down the levee into the river for a Viking burial. The least fun I ever had was seeing that car on the six o'clock news the next night, hanging from a crane, charges pending for obstructing a federal waterway.

I love that ol' river. I've seen my share of baptisms in the shallows, though how anybody thought they could be cleansed in such muddy water, I could never understand. I could ride the ferry all day long, and I can still feel the mud that cooled our feet in summer when we stood barefoot at the water's edge.

Sometimes I think my blood has river water in it. Just a touch of my pulse and I swear I can hear that ol' Mississippi calling me home.

My Mother's House

I stand at the door of my mother's house,
hand on the doorbell,
longing to hear the chimes
that once set dogs barking.
But what will I say if the new owner answers the door?

I could show him the patch of front yard
near the pecan tree,
where the white clover was always thickest—
where my sisters and I raced to see
who could catch the most honeybees
in the Ball jars our mother gave us.
We added grass and clover blossoms,
punched holes in the gold metal lids
so the bees could breathe,
dozed in the sweet grass
to their musical murmuring,
while the sun turned our skin
the color of honey.

I could point out the stand of longleaf pines
in the far corner of the backyard—
or what's left after sixty years of summer storms.
He's looked at them many times, of course,
but has he ever lain on the thick carpet
of lemon-scented needles in the middle of the copse,
thick with fairies dancing on every branch?

Over there's the wisteria that spills
across the bones of beloved family animals.
And the mimosa tree—Panther Girl's refuge
in times light and dark,

widespread limbs that welcomed me
to stretch out, bask, press my face into flowers,
drunk on the sweet scent of pink feather blossoms
and Louisiana summers.

My fingers press the bell.
The door opens.
Hello, I say. *I used to live here.*

My Father's Voice

1

At fourteen, he usually delivers
the evening paper by bicycle.
But today the Baton Rouge *State Times*
waits next to him on the porch,
neatly stacked. Mrs. Gilbert,
who dropped off the papers earlier,
pulls into the driveway a second time
to gather my uncle and his papers.
By the time they get to Rosemary's,
across from the little grocery store along his route
where he gets a pint of ice cream every day,
he is able to find his voice to tell his friend
his brother's been killed.

2

Black as India ink, darkness seeps
into my mother's womb.
Like a boat caught in a storm at sea,
I am flailing in embryonic fluid,
six weeks short of escape,
grief and loss laying their imprint
on my body and soul.
Though I listen for it, I can no longer
hear my father's voice.

3

Six decades later, I find his letters,
postmarks from Fort Knox, Vienna, Budapest.
His handwriting is elegant,

with perfectly rounded loops
barely able to contain his enthusiasm.
His letters lean left, as do his thoughts,
a liberal smattering of no-holds-barred fun!!!

While it's certain his hand will snap to attention
in the presence of his commanding officer,
his mind is always busy with girls,
weekend passes, black-market thrills,
and the things he'll write to his best friend
in the next letter about being 19,
in the U.S. Army, in Europe,
and the swell British girl he's met.

Now it's June—they're engaged—
and in December they will marry in London.
Everything is in order,
especially the lines on paper, the letters that,
though he has no inkling of it,
will reach across time
like strands of DNA
to let me know my father's voice again.

Sisters by Half

We didn't know the meaning of *half*
when we were young,
three little girls holding equal parts
of our mother's heart.
Different fathers, but our innocent eyes
could detect no difference
between biological and adopted love.

A beautiful net stretched over our home,
staked deep at the four corners of the yard,
a matrix of safety and boundaries
that jutted just a little
into Mrs. Hamilton's backyard,
where we played hide-and-seek
behind gigantic clumps of stinging pampas grass.
And though we scattered when we grew up,
the threads of mother-love kept us all
connected in a fragile web.

We found the cozies when she died,
a drawer full of blues and yellows,
creams and greens, knitted with tenderness
to make sure our tea would never grow cold.
But the unraveling had already begun.

The Fostoria stemware came to me,
and a few plates—*Mother's and my father's*—
all that remained of my parents' eleven months
together before the accident.
The forty-two years of everything else—
Mother's and their father's—
well, we did our best.

Tea is rare these days—
no place to go home to.
But family is more than shared DNA.
It's made of threads of light
that drop anchor in my heart
from sisters and brothers of spirit, too.

I find my eyes of innocence again—
so many connections between us all!
Blood, soul, karma, stars—
unbounded family,
everywhere we look.

The Turning

His shadow reaches me
all the way from Tennessee.
My uncle, the one who taught me
how to play "Chopsticks"
on my grandmother's piano when I was eight,
last thread connecting me
to the father I never knew.

Military man, pillar of the First Baptist,
his rich alto voice praises Jesus to the rafters
every Sunday morning.
His singing has to be loud,
to cover the sound of his soul
weeping at the man he has become.
You can feel his righteousness
even as he turns his back on me.

It was land that came between us,
a century of family property that held
everything I knew of my father.
The photo still standing on the dresser
in my grandmother's bedroom,
the places where I could trace his steps—
to the hen house, where he collected
warm eggs for his breakfast,
and through the wisteria
and Purple Dawn camellias,
where he and his brothers ran and laughed
and punched and loved one another.
Uncle wants it all, covers it all in blackness.

But like a sunflower reaching for the sky,
I cannot thrive in darkness.

I send my mind to the open field
where my father lay in the summer grass,
enchanted by tall green pines against blue space
and lazy as the drifting clouds.
I take comfort in the Light,
knowing that all are loved.

A Blue Field of Stars

The flag was perfect, a crisp triangle
with a blue field of shining stars,
a Flag of Remembrance to honor my father,
flown on Memorial Day, in the Healing Field,
in a small Tennessee town.

I pictured the soldiers who had lowered it,
thirteen folds made with ritual precision
by a creased and polished honor guard,
confident white-gloved hands, bugled taps,
the flag then offered to the living.

That's how they do it at military funerals,
for widows mourning their fallen husbands.
And that's how my uncle did it for me,
before either of us knew that his shadow would
one day stain all honor, all memory of goodness.

His betrayal drove me to the mall,
to the Victory Center, where I
pressed the flag into the hands
of a white-haired vet wanting to help,
uttered one word—*Please.*

He held the flag against his breast—
no need for words or history,
just a gentle smile,
and reverence, veneration.
Honor restored.

Pieces

She likes to glue things together,
make them whole again.
The slim porcelain vase, slender cylinder
of blue-green stems, purple and white iris,
twice broken, twice restored.

The silver-plated teaspoon from Belize,
whose crest falls off every once in a while.
The spotted leopard lamp that loses a tripod leg
every time it gets knocked off
the gold-leaf table in the entry hallway.

It's like that with family too.
Sometimes her heart breaks,
and she searches for a glue that
might mend the cracks of sorrow.
Greed and jealousy break bonds
once thought impenetrable.
Blood fails to triumph over power,
ugly untruths tear like shards of glass
across her breast.

But her heart whispers, *Look at the Light,*
and the shadowy fragments emerge,
each longing to be made whole.
Tender shoots of hope
supplant the darkness
as she realizes
nothing is ever truly broken.

2

LIFE AS A PRAYER

Life feels sacred to me, at least much of the time. I became a seeker of the sacred, and of truth, in my early twenties, when I was walking to work one morning in downtown Washington, D.C. and suddenly realized, *There must be more to life than this.* I walked into the Peace Corps headquarters, applied, got accepted, and headed for West Africa.

But the pull toward "something more" continued, and at the end of my two years as a volunteer, I headed for India, looking for a guru, or spiritual teacher. They say when the student is ready, the teacher appears—and mine was waiting for me. Enlightenment became my passion, my quest.

I had grown up Christian, but in India, I fell in love with several of the Hindu gods too, whom I understood to be overseers of various aspects of the One God's creation. I began meditating and learned to know the Self. I was blessed by saints and given a vision of life beyond this dimension. All of these influences serve me in a way that helps me always to find my way out of darkness into light and to see the divinity in all things.

Wild Child

I gave my soul a name.
Wild Child, I call her
or sometimes Sweet Child,
in the night.
Sugar, when I'm feeling Southern.

Wild was the girl
who lay in the white clover,
drunk on summer sun
and the clean smell of grass.
She'd roll onto her belly,
press her cheek against the ground,
cradled, like an infant
in the arc of its mother's neck,
fiercely protected, wildly content.

I want to lie with Life like this,
head resting on God's breast,
our pulses throbbing in unison,
fearless.

We can do this, Sugar.

Touchstone

Winter in the Deep South never lasted
more than four days at a time.
Those days, we walked to school
in thin little dresses
covered by thin little coats—
bare legs, bare hands, bare heads—
as if the thought of pants or gloves or hats
might appear concessional,
an invitation for winter to stay.

One day, squeezing my small frame smaller
against the cold, hands numb
clutching books and Cinderella lunchbox,
I made the painful three-block journey
from bus stop to home.
This is the coldest day of my life
and I'm NEVER *going to forget it.*
The shivery vow burned
into my six-year-old mind.

Awareness looks back,
recognizes Itself,
unchanging thread, child to elder.
Vibrating in the hum of the Eternal,
I feel the cold and laugh.

Sanctuary

For Martha Lemasters

She reached out
to catch me as I fell.
Let me help you, she urged,
completely at odds
with the hands-off, codependent-no-more
mentality reigning in my world.

She beckoned me to her home,
a Tolkien universe. Past the guard,
the trees were wondrous creatures—
twisting moss-covered live oaks,
palms in brilliant greens,
washed in a diffuse golden light,
like a filter of enchantment
in the hands of a skilled photographer.

The house was pure Florida, a postcard,
with a touch of Havana and Hemingway.
Inside, slow-moving ceiling fans,
dark, rich wood and wicker,
a writing desk that held a file
of inspiration just for me.

Her teaching was pure,
a new language that landed
in my eye of knowing,
wrapped itself around my thoughts,
and dropped into my throat and heart.
A shift from *asking* to *claiming,*
life as a prayer.

Easter Morning on Black Mountain

We were thinking of going to church
but first had to stick our noses out Candace's front door
to see if our Florida blood could meet the demands
of cold mountain air, chilled bones.

The first rays of sunlight, but there,
on the porch, a small square package,
wrapped in plain pink paper,
two fuchsia azaleas scotch-taped to the top.

Rose, Candace said, and showed us a photo
of her young friend, the mountain girl
who lived next door, just back
from a family trip to the Carolina shore.

Inside the box, four shells—
a calico scallop, a sundial, and a marsh periwinkle,
neatly stacked and covered
by the copper-colored back of a horseshoe crab.

I pictured the clear-eyed shell seeker
reaching down to examine a moon snail
while other 12-year-olds clutched their phones,
felt a surge of hope.

Goodness, gentleness, and love
in a little pink box,
a perfect sermon for Easter morning
on Black Mountain.

The Yogini

She eases into Triangle Pose,
feet wide, hugging the tangerine mat,
arms wide awake, stretching
between heaven and earth
like a tilted Vitruvian man.

She checks her alignment—
imperceptible shift of hips—
presses her back body gently
against an imagined plane.

Her gaze rides an outflow of breath
upward to her reaching hand,
follows the line of light
from fingertips to the point
at the center of the celestial arc.

Heart open, she breathes in the stars.

Black Ivory

She was looking for the yellow sapphire
that clips on to her short strand of pearls
when she came across the ivory ring,
a trinket she'd bought decades earlier
for a few francs in the humming market
of Porto Novo.

Two years in West Africa,
a love affair with the bush,
utter ignorance of the sacrifice
behind the creamy beauty.

She stands at the water's edge,
waiting for the moon to rise.
She studies the tiny circle,
twisted like braided bread,
kisses the ring to kiss the elephant.

She holds it up with both hands,
like a priest offering the communion wafer,
and prays, *Wash the blood from this ring*
and the black stain from history and my soul.

Then she hurls the ring into the ocean,
into the loving arms of the Great Mother.

Balancing Act

1.

In a teaching moment, my father asked
whether I loved him or my mother more.
And which of my two little sisters?
I could see his point.
Then he asked which hand I liked best.
Left, I said, baffling us both.

My love of the left followed me into adulthood.
A preference for left-brain logic and structure.
A liberal lifestyle, left-leaning politics.
Sleeping to the left of my husband.
Even the word feels softer in my mouth
than the tight, hard *right*.

2.

At the workshop, we held hands in a circle,
left palm up to receive, right palm down to give.
Left is the goddess, we were taught—
it receives, surrenders, asks for help.

3.

My left side is under attack.
Broken bones, misalignments,
small dark shadows under my arm,
which handsome, lavender-gowned surgeons
now cut away.
A crack in the feminine.

A cry for help and light streams
from my brothers and sisters
around the world, weaving itself
into a silky hammock
that holds, cradles, soothes.
Protection falls like a blanket
from the celestial realms.
I rest in a matrix of invisible hands.

The Wedding

What is left to say at the wedding
after fifteen years together,
what is left to marry?

Medicine woman, the thought flashed
the instant I first saw you.
So different, we two,
yet our hands closed perfectly
around each other.

Fingers entwined, we walked for years
along sandy beaches,
to set our feet in one direction.
We lay on our backs in Atlantic waters,
grasping hands in the vastness,
surrendering conflict to the currents
sweeping out to sea.

You made medicine from gemstones,
and we swallowed diamonds, white sapphires,
drinking ourselves into a state of beauty
that withstood all loss and sorrow.

Now here we stand,
in the Christ garden,
inside a sacred wood.
The ceremony begins.
A thousand bamboo stalks
quiver in ecstasy.

Imprinted

Saraswati is the Hindu goddess of knowledge, music, art, and wisdom. "Holy One" refers to the beloved saint Karunamayi, who is revered as an incarnation of this goddess.

The Holy One inscribes the mantra
on my tongue with a twig
from the sacred tulsi plant.
Then she lifts my writing hand,
traces the Sanskrit letters across my palm.

Saraswati breathes herself into me,
paints my throat with honey
so every word that rises from my heart
comes out sweet and good,
like the high, clear notes of a flute.

Her music is in all things—
the warbler's notes falling from the oaks
like thistle scattered from the feeder;
the gentle purring of sandhill cranes
resting in their night places by the pond;
unhurried voices over morning coffee
floating from a neighbor's balcony;
whistles, sirens, humming engines.

Goddess, if I am to be your voice,
let music be my language too,
like the exhale of the wind
that rattles the palm fronds,
a thousand tiny crystal chimes.

The Hill at Medjugorje

Hail, Mother, full of grace, Power is with Thee.

Against the sky I watch you climb,
looking for me in the tops of firs,
in rosaries, in fervent prayers,
hungering for a glimpse of me.
But I hunger for you more.

Blessed are you, Queen of the Universe,
and blessed is all of creation.

You think your seeking is new,
but I have been with you from the beginning,
walked with you since you were a child.
I hear your cries.

Holy Mother, maker of all things,

Your yearning rips the sky around me.
You weep for your dead friend,
your bankrupt business,
gasping for breath like a runner
at the end of the race.
You search the workplace,
the marketplace, your children's faces,
desperate for some honoring
of who you think you are—
but you have lost more
than your children and your job.
I lean my face toward you.

Be with us now and always, Blessed Be!

Listen to my whisper: *I am here!*
At the top of the hill,
in the pain in your chest,
in perfect reflection, blue robes to blue jeans.

Raise your arms high above your head
that I may take your hands in mine.
Your pain will lift you into the sky.
Finally you will say *Yes!*
knowing I am your breath.

Hail, Mother, full of grace, Power is with Thee.

Quan Yin

Quan Yin is worshipped as the female aspect of Buddha.
She is known as the Goddess of Compassion and Mercy.

I did not lay joss sticks at your feet
when I was a child, nor flowers,
did not bend before you with folded hands.
But I needed something for the shelf
inside my front door,
and I found you.

At first a decoration, your statue graced the hall,
round-cheeked goddess with slanted eyes,
white light reflecting off alabaster robes.
I loved the pearls dangling from your neck,
the exquisite lines of your nose
curving into perfect arches above half-closed eyes.

You seemed so busy,
blessing this and that
with your porcelain hands,
robes carved to swing and sway
as you moved, bare feet dancing
on demons unable to stand
in the face of such beauty.

They call you Goddess of Compassion,
and that was what I wanted—
to see through eyes of mercy,
know the secret of half-smiles.
I tried to catch your eye,
but your mind seemed somewhere else.

So I followed your gaze inward,
like the curve of a petal on a white orchid,
beyond compassion, beyond mercy,
all the way to stillness.

A thousand names for the Divine Mother,
but you, Quan Yin, have found me.

The Elephant God

Ganesh, the elephant god, is one of most worshipped deities among Hindus. He is known as the remover of obstacles.

I found him in the gift shop
by the Indian restaurant on Long Island
the night before my surgery—
three inches of white alabaster,
vermillion ears and trunk,
ruby-red garland around his neck,
golden arcs and jewels covering his body,
a diamond at his third eye.

The surprising thing about an elephant—
as I learned while riding on the back
of one in the jungle of South India—
is the utter quietness in which he travels.
You expect the ground to thunder,
but there is only silence
radiating from his giant heart,
punctuated by the sound of twigs
snapping beneath his padded, oversize feet
as he carries you through thick trees
with ease and grace.

Jai Ganesha, jai Ganesha, jai Ganesha deva,
I sing to the elephant god.
From the dark and twisting forests
to the sparkling star belts circling the sky,
I ride upon your muscled back,
carried across the silent stones of life.
If I slip off, it is only to kneel
before your red-white-and-gold majesty,
to bask in your beauty and compassion,
to rest in your wisdom and omnipotence.

Ganga

The River Ganges, called Ganga, is considered India's holiest river, worshipped as a goddess.

I hear the river before I see her,
water slapping concrete
at the foot of the stair-stepped *ghat*
where I sit waiting for first light.

A dream, this River Ganga,
that robbed me of sleep all the way
from Kathmandu to ancient Varanasi.
Eighteen hours over washboard roads
on a cartoon of a bus piled high
with luggage, hens, goats,
Nepalese leaning out of windows,
and me, hungry for something sacred.

Splashing water now, and puja bells,
as dawn breaks the darkness
to reveal half-naked men
scooping, pouring, praying.
Light ripples on the gold-black water.
I rest in the arms of the goddess.

In the Saint's Tent

For Anandamayi Ma,
"India's most perfect flower"

The wave started at the back of the open tent,
a sea of people rolling forward
to flatten their bodies against the ground.
The Holy One was approaching.
She took her seat but did not speak.

Out of chaos, a line—a single file
of devotees pressing forward.
Place your offerings here, but do not touch Mother,
the two guardians flanking her
instructed each person *in their own language.*

Suddenly, it was my hands
placing fruits and flowers
on the simple brass tray before her.
I fell to my knees, and when I arose,
accepted the tangerine placed in my hand.

Dazzled, I made my way
out of the shaded tent
into the brilliant morning sun.
I peeled the precious fruit,
devoured divinity.

Surgical Vision

She filled me with her blue-diamond essence,
promised protection—
I will be at your head,
my son, the Christ, at your feet.

She introduced my celestial guardians—
Lithusia, standing on my left
in raiment of dawn blue edged in navy,
Anna Mae to my right in light-suffused rose.
Large angels, she added.

St. Germain will be your surgeon,
and at my request,
Archangel Raphael will hold us all
in the healing of sacred time and space.

She was right about all of it.
Not even the veil of anesthesia
could block the grace of these light beings
from permeating my body and soul.
They came and have not left.

Kumbha Mela 1974

The Kumbha Mela is the largest religious festival in the world, held every three years in rotation at four sacred Hindu sites around India, each situated on one or more holy rivers. Bathing in one of these rivers during the weeks-long event is thought to be auspicious due to astrological events and the holiness of the rivers, but to bathe at the most auspicious astrological moment during that time is believed to guarantee enlightenment in this lifetime.

Only eighteen kilometers from Rishikesh to Haridwar,
but it took us three hours to get there.
An endless line of cars clung to the edge
of the mountain, ascending the narrow ribbon
of road into the Himalayas.

Every pilgrim, saint, and sadhu,
yogi, ascetic, and mendicant
moved with single mind
into the valley of the Ganges.
A hundred million people yearning
to kiss the feet of God.

Our small band of devotees
was about to be crushed,
caught up in a tsunami of people
surging toward the river and the auspicious hour.
But we had come here with a saint.
Satyanand—"true bliss"—
with long silver hair and white beard,
the white silk *dhoti* of the *bramachari.*

In an instant, space-time seemed to bend itself,
and at the holy moment—exactly 2:38 am—
we slipped through the wormhole,
straight into the swiftly flowing current
of baptismal waters.

The sun was already rising by the time
I climbed to the roof of the house
where saints and seekers now rested.
I unrolled my sleeping bag
but didn't bother to unzip it—
I always loved turning back
the Egyptian blue cover to reveal
the scarlet red lining,
but it was already too hot.
My waist-length hair and sari
had dried quickly in the night heat,
and I lay down, fully clothed,
in the quiet companionship of strangers.

My young bones relaxed easily
into the concrete floor,
and the promise of enlightenment
followed me into my dreams.

Swiss Moon

For Maharishi Mahesh Yogi

In winter, the spruce and silver firs
dressed in silent snow and moonlight.
I sat at the feet of the guru.

Summer bloomed in alpine meadows
of gentian and edelweiss,
rejoicing in sunlight, seduced by the moon.
I kissed the feet of my guru.

Let's go for a boat ride, the guru said,
and we rode his laughter
into the middle of the night
and the middle of Lake Lucerne,

where the moon cast her net of white-silver
and laid claim to us all.

Tracks

For Ron

When inward tenderness finds the secret hurt,
pain itself will crack the rock and let the soul emerge.
—Rumi

Long before the ground begins to shake,
you can hear the trains.
Wheels clack over old tracks,
whistles blare their warnings—
two longs, one short, one long—
train language, all night.

Ten days since you laid your body on the rails,
let the Burlington Northern Santa Fe
rip your soul into the afterlife.
I breathe the earth,
try to imagine your final thoughts.

Was your face turned toward the stars that night,
or did you search the ground
for the bones of your Cherokee ancestors?
Could you feel the trembling of the rails,
or was it your own fragile bones that quaked?
Did your mind travel to a faraway place
so you could pretend this was not your choice?
Did you cry for God at the rending
of the space-time fabric?

The *Polar Express* has returned
in time for Christmas, trailing stars.
My grandchild sits for hours inside his track circle,
lining up the cars of his little toy train,
pushing, pulling, spilling them across the tracks.
Then, laughing, he picks up the pieces,
starts all over again.

Toward Home

In the rehab center

Stargazer lilies stare at her
across the small, sterile room,
fuchsia-and-white imprints
in the soul space behind her eyes.

In the hallway, incessant beeping,
monitors throbbing in time with the pain
pulsing in her broken bones.
Make it stop, she pleads,
but nobody answers the call light.

She makes friends, and enemies.
An aide slips her extra orange juice.
A nurse sneaks pain meds early
in case of emergency.

But raucous staff party in the night.
Massive machines clean floors at 4:30 a.m.,
construction on the new rooms begins at midnight.
It's a rehab center, not a place to rest,
they tell her when she begs for mercy.

She turns to the roses from Singapore,
peach and cream, delicious emissaries
from her far-away daughter.
Her room becomes a swirling vortex of beauty—
handmade cards from the mountains,
packages with treats and art magazines,
books of poems and mystery.

Lunch arrives with friends,
tenderness is texted.

Her lover brings tea
and a china cup from home.

In her dreams, an orderly offers coffee
in her grandmother's floral demitasse cup,
her fingers clutch at little levers
to lock her wheelchair in place.
Body and soul, practicing to go home.

Savannah's Table

Savannah is one of my nicknames.

Tea at my house at 2:15,
I tell my girlfriends' answering machines.
Through the back door into the sunroom
women flock to my table
like goldfinches to the feeder,
attached to kids and diaper bags,
lovers, ex-husbands, groceries pulling.
But, by God, they will have tea
at Savannah's table today.

Queens, they sip honey-colored amber
from my best china, fine-boned, translucent.
Silver teaspoons stir their stories,
rest on beds of lilacs and roses.
Slender hands finger shortbread,
mince pies even Buckingham Palace
would welcome, they tell me,
stilled for an instant by the taste of love.

Then they lift again the cups
that hold my heart.

3

SIMPLE THINGS

I find happiness in simple things. Broken shells on the beach, an empty calendar day, English tea, palm trees. I find great beauty—even a holiness—in colors, sounds, and scents. My partner's face and hands.

But I was not always simple. Driven by an urge to succeed, I once found myself trapped by the demands of fame, headed for a nervous breakdown. I watched friends and colleagues always wanting more, never satisfied, and began to ask myself, *What is enough?*

Through Grace, I was able to recognize that I had enough. That I *was* enough.

Miss Lee High '65

Miss Lee High had a singular purpose,
a long list of clubs and awards
after her name in the senior yearbook.
"... accomplishments give lustre"—
the quote next to the shining image
of the girl Most Likely to Succeed.

She rode Success into adulthood
like a race horse, driven by an urge to win
that left quirt marks on her soul.
Pauses for marriage, children,
but so much to do!
She never stopped to wonder
what the finish line might look like.

She broke under the weight of her in-box one day,
an utter collapse, a near-death experience,
the only sound the ripping away
of the mask on the face of illusion.

She returned in a new dream.
Spaces on her calendar, in her mind,
her heart an open field of possibility.
No more wanting.
She was everything she needed.

Simple Things

The book promised a hundred ways
to slow down and simplify my life,
but the first page I turned to
suggested planting a garden
to reduce trips to the grocery store.
I quickly returned it to its place,
pulled three Mary Olivers from my shelves.

Mary Oliver might have planted a garden—
but the idea wouldn't have come from a book.
She would have met a patch of soil near the woods,
listened carefully as it begged her
to dig her hands into its coolness.
Tiny seeds would have entered her vision,
pinpricks of light in the dark earth.
Later, the garden would find itself
awash in gratitude as she gathered
the bounty offered by each herb and flower.

I will not plant a garden today.
But I will be thoughtful about the words I write.
I will notice the ease in my body,
savor the unfolding of an empty day.
Bow to the simple things.

Beneath the Radar

Some of my friends are famous.
They might dine with a European princess,
share the stage with Sir Richard Branson,
be granted an audience with the Dalai Lama.

I slipped into a smaller life.
A tiny sliver at the edge of the continent.
Why go to India when my eyes can travel
all the way to Earth's curve in no-time,
2.9 miles from my sea-striped beach chair
across rolling, breathing, Atlantean aquamarine.

My thoughts are like breaths now.
They rise, then fall into stillness,
like the gap at the end of an exhale.
I am in love with this quiet place.
It lets me hear the palm trees singing.
It writes my poems.

Memorial Day

The sea had laid a carpet of broken shells
across the sand, a billion memorials
to fallen creatures of the deep.
Her feet reveled in the rough texture,
while her eyes sought the softness
of conch-colored pinks, her favorites
except for the pieces of alabaster white,
smooth and stained with amethyst.

Low tide, and the snowbirds
had fled for the summer,
the beach a luxury of emptiness.
How do you stand the heat?
they always wanted to know.

She leaned down to finger a ridged fragment
of pink shell, an angel's wing
that she slipped into her pocket,
a marker, like a thousand others,
of a day she wanted to remember.

Out of Bounds

In a dream, she unzipped her skin suit,
stepped out of her soul-home,
floated, widened, rose.
A few flyovers, fast and low
like the Blue Angels,
then she settled into orbit,
studied the dwelling below.

At once, seven billion heartbeats
vibrated her body in a pulse of singularity.
She could smell the scent of newborns
washed clean by their mothers,
taste the sweetness dripping from honeysuckle vines,
hear the wings of a trillion butterflies.

The only divides she could see
between blue and red
were sapphire and cerulean river ribbons
that cut through brick-colored deserts,
the red clay of Mississippi,
the burning rocks of Zion.

In the morning, when she landed,
she opened the door onto a new world.

Authors Ridge

Authors Ridge is a section of Sleepy Hollow Cemetery in Concord, Massachusetts.

The names on the stones
at the top of the hill
are noble—Emerson,
Thoreau, Alcott, Hawthorne.
So little space their bodies take,
sons and daughters asleep
for ages with their families,
giants in simple graves,
marked by the offerings
of wayfarers—pens, pencils,
scribbled lines of favorite verses.

It's quiet in Sleepy Hollow,
but on Authors Ridge, no death.
Words flash between tombstones,
as the voices of the great writers
reach across the centuries
to tell their tales of little women,
scarlet letters, Walden Pond,
the Revolution.

I place my pen across Louisa May's name,
joy in my pilgrim's heart.

Secret Beach

I lay in bed that night
feeling the tide in my body,
a rolling of blood,
as if I were still suspended
in the salty ocean water.

The dolphins had surprised us that day,
arriving before we could reach
the far end of the deserted beach.
Overcome by madness,
we flung our gear to the ground,
tore across the burning sand,
fumbled with fins in the crashing surf,
kicked our way through the violent backwash
into cool, deep water.

We settled into yogi breath,
slow sounds through the snorkel
guiding us out to sea as far as we dared—
an imaginary line to the Kilauea lighthouse
the boundary where we tread water and waited.

And then they were there,
circling, surrounding, under, around us.
Majestic. Ecstatic.

Back in bed, my dream self flies into the sky,
takes in the island's edge—
lace-leafed trees against the cliff,
half-moon arc of white silk sand
curving into the outcropping
with its tiny lighthouse at the end—
endless blue-green ocean,

and two specks far from shore,
naked white-brown bodies
floating alone in vast wildness.

My body trembles.

The Beauty of Him

He was left alone in his wheelchair
at the edge of the physical therapy room,
head bowed, broken.
She studied him as she willed her legs
to lift the weights around her ankles.

About seventy, she guessed,
and he looked like a great don.
Silver hair combed straight back
from his honey-colored face,
gray designer jeans and matching hoodie

over a spotless white shirt,
sandals with wide, crisscrossing bands
a shade lighter than his golden skin.
I want to meet him, she thought,
and slipped onto her own wheels
to roll across the floor.

Mr. Sanchez, she said. His head lifted.
She rested her hand lightly on his arm,
took in the beauty of him.
I love the way you look.

He can't see you, the therapist said,
and he speaks only Portuguese.
But the old man covered her hand
with his and smiled.

Magnolias at the Mall

Nothing on the calendar today.
No answers to prepare
for the latest court pleading,
no proofs of claim to file
against the white-collar dream thieves,
no ozone therapy to pump life
into misshapen cells.

Perhaps I'll go check on the row
of tall magnolias, elegant guards
at the entrance to the mall.
Or maybe I'll lie in ocean foam
for a while, take a cue from the children
too young to read the warnings—
Drop-off! Shore break! Rip currents!—
fearless under their mother's gaze.

Actually, it's a perfect day
to go next door to John's,
rest in the garden,
drink the whiteness of gardenias.

What I Mean by Love

1.

The first time I saw you, beloved,
my heart cried and leapt—
Who is that medicine woman?
Light bounced off the angled plane
of your cheekbones,
silver hair flowed to your waist.
Your gaze was steady, as was your gait,
as if you walked barefoot on the earth,
not shoe-clad on concrete.
Your skin looked like the Mediterranean sun,
flashing images of Van Gogh's olive orchards
in the South of France.

2.

The morning I met him in the hallway,
the windows of my beloved guru's
Mumbai apartment were thrown wide
to catch the ocean breezes,
sounds of the street vendors
and snake charmers rising from below.
I tried to step aside,
but his ancient, gnarled hands reached up,
his arms encircled, pulled me
into a pool of Grace.

3.

Slipping into the dream space last night,
I heard the Great Horned Owl calling her mate—

three short notes, two long—a bird Morse Code.
After a while, he responded, a third interval lower
but the same dots and dashes,
telegraphed across the live oaks
like the call-and-response
of a priest and his congregation.
The duet quickened, their voices overlapping
until they flew out of my dream.

In Search of Mary Oliver

1.

A few lines of Mary Oliver,
and she begins to cry.
Her own morning light
doesn't fall on coreopsis—
it highlights the neighbor's car
encroaching on her parking space.
She can't hear birds' wings overhead—
high-impact windows protect
against hurricanes and Florida heat
and every sweet sound of birds and tree frogs.

2.

When she was a child, a hurricane meant
a sleepover at her best friend's house.
Her parents let them stand on the veranda,
watch the winds lash the oak trees,
feel the spray of wind-whipped water,
twirl their bodies in a whirlwind of glee.
She spent half her childhood
face down in pink clover,
white pine needles, breathing dirt.

3.

November. The in-between time,
when you can throw open the house,
inhale the smell of sunlight
before the heat stifles every thought.
A few lines of Mary Oliver
and she unlatches every door and window,

listens as the house fills with music—
cardinals, jays, mourning doves.

She resolves to go to the beach,
count the brown pelicans flying south,
lie on the sand beside a sea turtle's nest,
feel the heartbeat of a hundred babies
waiting to be born.

Another Flower

The flowers were from her ex-husband,
a small white card visible
among the iris and stargazer lilies
he knew she loved—*Thank you for being*
a wonderful mother to my children—
the same message, year after year.
She never minded that the iris peaked
and died before the lilies even got started.

She had done her best.
Babies were her childhood dream.
She pretend-nursed her dolls,
lovingly changed their sweet little dresses,
hand-sewn by her own mother.

But at seventeen, a life sentence—
there would be no children.
Grief, then she adjusted her emotions,
embraced the freedom of an absent womb,
relished a life unfettered by family.

But sometimes love is a package deal.
She informed her husband-to-be
that his children would *never* live with them.

Son moved in at thirteen.
They circled each other like wary lions,
setting boundaries, marking territories.
Two battles in two weeks, her legs wobbling
in the face of his righteous anger.

But the unnatural mother knew exactly
how to protect the young cub,
and he fell willingly into the fierceness

of her safety net.
They learned how to look after each other.

He calls to thank her for being a great mom
and to tell her first, *We're having a baby.*
Another flower for Mother's Day.

Colors of a Different Kind

Sometimes I feel like Michelangelo.
I'm no painter, but I know well
the colors of agony and ecstasy.

My ex-husband calls to say
he might have cancer.
I play Atticus Finch—
It's not time to worry yet—
as bile reaches the back of my throat.

My own cancer is gone—
surgeons tore open my flesh
but couldn't find the darkness
they were looking for.
I ache for answers.

My daughter's family is crumbling
on the other side of the world.
My hand longs to reach
through my computer screen
to smooth the strain on her face.

Yet simple moments come to me.
It's -3 in the Midwest where I used to live,
but I walk the beach
in thin shorts and T-shirt,
ocean foam cooling my bare feet.

Every morning, just before breakfast,
an invisible woodpecker jackhammers
an oak outside my balcony.
A Spanish guitar or Snatam Gaur
singing *Ray Man Shabad*

causes my throat to widen,
releasing a primal sound
of awe and wonder
at the ineffable beauty of life.

Florida Forecast

The forecast is calling for sunshine
today, tomorrow, the rest of eternity.
The cardinals have gone mad,
the geese are raising a ruckus on the pond.

I open my mouth to join the praise,
to let out the light shaping itself
between my breasts and announcing,
like the Star of Bethlehem,
Something great is happening here!

The sun, wearing his magician's hat,
coaxes new green out of flat, gray branches,
nudges flowers out of their buds,
invites me to sweep winter off the porch.

"Building" is the word of the day
for mourning doves and squirrels,
man-boys with their dump trucks
moving dirt and making way.

The evening news reminds us
of the snow we used to shovel,
the ice we busted tailbones on,
the shrinking of winter bodies,
as if becoming smaller might make us invisible.

But the news ends, sunlight pours
into us like a blessing, and as usual,
the weatherman has got it right.

Exotica

The palm trees are blossoming,
seeding themselves on wind and wings
along the lush Treasure Coast.

Queens drip with golden necklaces,
their court a thousand honeybees.

King Alexander drops creamy stalks
of amethyst petals like streamers
from his crown, while Pinanga palms

push white kernels out of their spathes,
hanging like rows of perfect pearls
that shine against coral branches.

Royals spill their white flowers
over the ground, covering it
like a gentle snow.

This morning, I caught a scent
like jasmine in the south of India.
Then I remembered the date palm
below my window, a virile male
with ivory strands of tiny fragrant stars
looking for females to woo.

Who can get anything done
with all this exotic beauty
and the air filled with trees
loving one another?

Leaving the Blue Ridge Mountains

It was like driving through a Seurat painting,
a river of asphalt between banks of dense trees,
every leaf a dot of thick color—
electric limes, pistachios, fern and olive greens,

April yellows—not the somber mustards
and corn golds of fall, but bright canary yellows,
lemons and bumblebees,
accented by the hunter green of towering pines.

At home, a single row of coconut palms
welcomed me at the beach.
Monsieur Gaugin, I thought,
as I waved to my familiar friends.

The whole Earth, it seems, is the sketchbook
of a very fine Artist.

Five A.M.

Stillness wraps her like soft silk.
Nothing moves but first light,
a skillful artist this morning,
unveiling images out of darkness
the way Michelangelo freed figures from marble.

She puts the kettle on,
prepares her tea tray—
the Wedgewood teapot covered in peonies,
the delicate Princess Margaret Rose cup,
with yellow parakeets and robin's egg edges,
the silver teaspoon with the crest of London,
the pink-and-white pitcher from Wimbledon,
which she fills with heavy cream.

She carries the whistling kettle
across the kitchen to the pot—
not the other way around,
her British grandmother always insisted—
warms the teapot, pours boiling water
over fragrant black leaves from England,
her grandmother's favorite.
The cream-and-green tea cozy
her mother knitted slips over the pot.

She pours a cup of amber goodness,
drinks in the morning.

Old Photos

She tosses the old photos into the bin
as if they were just another
newspaper or envelope headed to recycling.
I pull them out, one by one,
study the faces of my partner
as child.

She would have been my best friend.
We'd have relished summers,
ruling the neighborhood
on our chariot bikes.
We'd have cooled our hot heads
in New England ponds,
explored the woods until we knew
every patch of berries,
where the poison ivy grew.
We'd have reigned like monarchs,
crowns of clover on our heads,
fearless together.

I ache for the beauty of her youth.
I long to know her when we were six
and fourteen and twenty-five.
I want to marry her at thirty,
cement our lives and celebrate
our anniversary fifty years later.

But we were given to each other
in the second half of life.
We must work quickly
to know each other well.
There will never be enough time,
and I want to get inside the heart,

touch the innocence, the eagerness
on the face of that little girl
in the old photos.

D Street

I'm on D Street, she loved to announce
from the car, voice bright as a star
on a clear Iowa night.
Then an excited recitation—
what she'd bought at the farmers market,
how many deer she'd startled at Jefferson County Park,
which mulberry trees had let loose their bounty.

D Street. Code for *our street, almost home.*
Or *I got something especially for you.*
Or *I gathered silence at the park today*
and can't wait to share it with you.

Across the country, we live on a boulevard now.
The park is riverside—no deer, no berries.
But she still calls on her way home from anywhere.
I'm on D Street, she tells me,
only five minutes away
but unable to contain the joy
of impending reunion.

Flower Child

The day we hitchhiked into San Francisco
from the East Coast, Jefferson Airplane
was playing at Fillmore West.
Pinch me, I'm dreaming,
thought the girl with bellbottoms
and perfect hippie hair down to her waist.
I'd have gone down any rabbit hole
with Gracie Slick.

We lived on good vibrations—
hashish, peyote, Acapulco Gold—
but music was our soul.
Lennon, Dylan, Stills, the Dead,
their rallying cries of peace
carried us across the currents
of change and raging passion,
a sturdy ship on a turbulent ocean.

The leaders of the band are dying now—
Kantner, Cocker, BB King, and Frey.
Each passing stirs a memory—
Woodstock, Washington, the streets of Chicago.
And the music,
ever-flowing from my lips.

Taking My Measurements

I wonder if on my deathbed
I'll have time to calculate
the exact midpoint of my life—
reflect on where I was at that moment
and what I was doing, oblivious
that I had just completed
the first half of my life.

If this seems weird, just know that
I get immense pleasure from measuring things,
like how long it takes to make the king-size bed—
two minutes, in case you're wondering.

Or counting the number of stairs
from my condo at the top of the building
to the ground floor—two flights of eighteen,
I should add, which always makes me feel
triumphant when I go the other way
and labor at the top for only six breaths.

This is good to know because I remember
hearing about two Indian astrologers
visiting the town where I used to live,
aghast to see a runner flying by
as they were on their evening stroll—
Doesn't he know that life is measured
in breaths?

That explains a lot, but on second thought,
I don't think I'll be measuring much
on my deathbed. If I'm lucky,
I'll be looking into the eyes of my beloved,
staring at the face of Love—
infinite, timeless, and utterly immeasurable.

Crepe-Paper Dreams

How beautiful it is to do nothing,
and then rest afterward.
—Spanish Proverb

They told me I couldn't retire—
the world needed my gifts
and I'd be lost without purpose, meaning.

I thought about long-ago Christmas mornings,
peeling layers of crepe-paper streamers
from the surprise balls in our stockings
in the hunt for coins and trinkets.
I wanted to unravel myself like that,
all the way to the main prize at center.

I set out to unlearn life.
I put down my phone.
Practiced witnessing the impulse
to go to my desk—and not moving.
Breaths became longer, softer,
and the slow, flowing movements
of Tai Chi began to inhabit my body.

You might not see it from the outside,
but inside, a Buddha smile.
If someone asks what I'm doing these days,
I just tell them, feeling good.

ACKNOWLEDGMENTS

I gratefully acknowledge the editors of the following publications, in which some of these poems first appeared, sometimes in slightly different form:

Amore: Love Poems: "Old Photos"

Soul-Lit: A Journal of Spiritual Poetry: "Ripening," "Touchstone," "D Street," "Sanctuary" (originally titled "A New Language")

On the Veranda Literary Journal: "Close to the Ground," "My Mother's House"

Painting the Eucalyptus Midnight: "Author's Ridge," "Ganesh," "The Forecast"

I also wish to express my deepest gratitude to the following people:

To Diane Frank, founder of Blue Light Press and a beautiful writer, poet, and editor, whom I am fortunate to call teacher and friend.

To the women of the Blue Light Press poetry workshops, my Poet Sisters, whose invaluable feedback encourages, lifts, and inspires me to hone this craft: Suzanne Dudley-Schon, Anna Kodama, Lisha Garcia, Angie Minkin, Nancy Lee Melmon, and Kathryn Goldman.

To the women of the Durham, NC writers group Quill and Brush, who generously included me in this year's annual retreat: Pamela George, Marian Place, Kendy Madden,

Carolyn Kroll, and Nancy Henderson-James. I'm grateful for the wise input of these professionals, in whose presence this collection was born.

To Karla Cristensen, my first poetry teacher, for shepherding me into the world of poetry writing.

To Billy Collins, Poet Laureate of the United States from 2001 to 2003, for his online poetry master class, from which I learned so much.

To Elizabeth "Lilli" Botchis, my life partner, for everything.

ABOUT THE AUTHOR

Jennifer Read Hawthorne is the author/editor of seven books, including the #1 *New York Times* best sellers *Chicken Soup for the Woman's Soul* and *Chicken Soup for the Mother's Soul.* Together, her books have sold more than 14 million copies.

Jennifer lives in Vero Beach, Florida, with her life partner, Elizabeth, nourished by palm trees and ocean. This is her first book of poetry.

www.jenniferhawthorne.com
jennifer@jenniferhawthorne.com

Made in the USA
Lexington, KY
01 December 2019